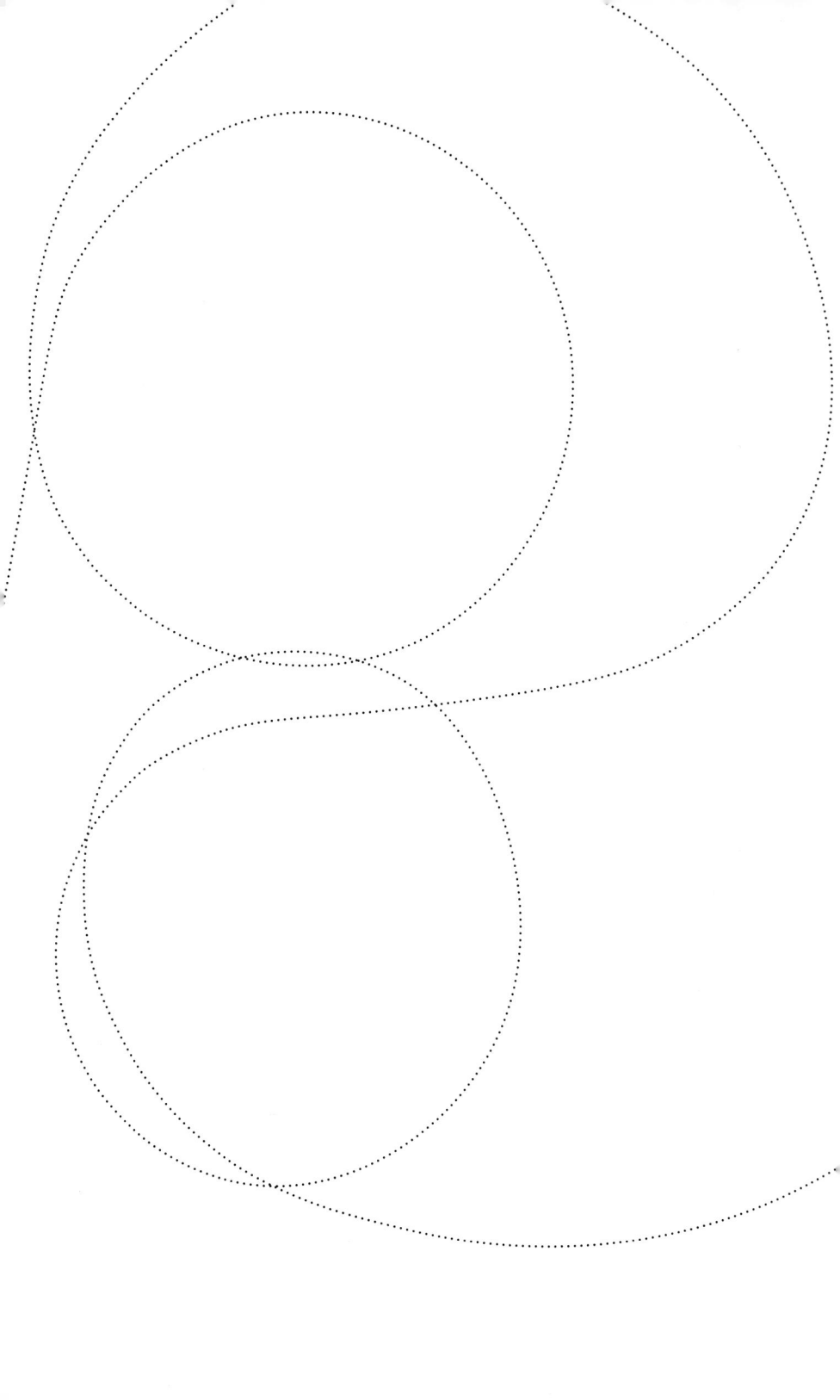

The Neighbourhood

Hannah Lowe

Published by Out-Spoken Press,
Future Studio,
237 Hackney Road,
London, E2 8NA

First edition published 2019

ISBN: 978-1-9996792-2-4

Design & Art Direction: Kate Austin

Printed & Bound by: Print Resource

Typeset in: Baskerville

Out-Spoken Press is supported using public
funding by the National Lottery through Arts
Council England.

Supported using public funding by
LOTTERY FUNDED | **ARTS COUNCIL
ENGLAND**

Acknowledgements

Thanks to the editors of the following publications where some of these poems or versions of them have appeared: *Compass, Paris Lit Up, Poetry London, Prairie Schooner, Rialto, Soundings, The Caught Habits of Language: An Entertainment for W.S. Graham for Him Having Reached One Hundred.*

'Total Body Conditioning' was a commission for R.A.P Party at Kings Place, 2018. 'The Garden is Not for Everyone' was written for the online project *New Boots and Pantisocracies: 100 days of poetry for the austere generation.* 'Deportation Blues' draws on Luke de Noronha's writing about violent deportation to Jamaica (https://twitter.com/LukeEdeNoronha)

These poems were written during my residency at Keats House, the theme of which was 'the neighbourhood'.

Many thanks, as ever, to Mimi Khalvati and RFH group; to the Torriano group; to Richard Scott and Richard Price.

for Rory, and the neighbourhood

Contents

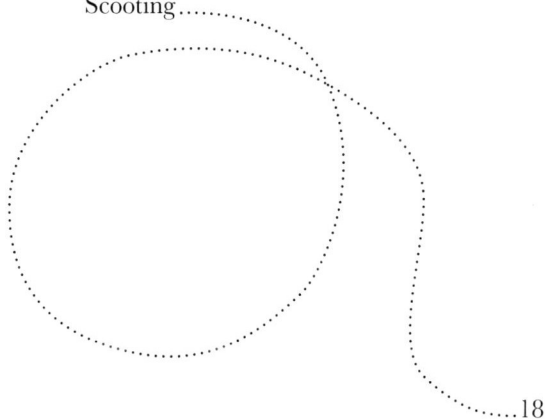

My mother groan'd! my father wept.
Into the dangerous world I leapt...

'Infant Sorrow', William Blake

The Blue Door

In the dream, the phone in my bag tells me
my baby is crying. I am somewhere in the city
riding the night train. The phone bleeps
in my hand, the train rolls to a stop
I see my baby standing in his cot
his face wet, a red knot

In the dream, I yank open
the carriage doors, I run
down tracks, down the black iron steps
to the old neighbourhood – the shops
all boarded up, a fired-out car
crows swooping the empty square
I turn each corner, crazy
Which house has my baby?

In the dream, I push open a tall blue door
everything inside how I left it before
a pool of dresses on the tiles
that syrup smell
the buzz of flies
I stand there, listening for my baby's cry –

The Fence

I had no Greek, so couldn't ask

    about the carrier bags she tended,

six strung from the mangled oak

    four spilling from an upstairs sill,

all corner-shop blue. She'd climb

    the steps, barefoot in her tights,

loosen their knots, peer in

    at what? Something bulky and earthy

I could see, like beetroot

    but why hang beetroot from a tree?

When the baby began to show

    she came shyly to the fence,

sun in her white hair, her palm

    laid flat on her sunken womb,

she said *my son* then *doctor*

    pointing up over the chimneys

to the world beyond the gardens

    where I pictured him in a pristine office,

efficient, handsome, fluent.

    If I could have asked her more I would:

How long had she lived there?

    Why did her husband park up outside

for hours? Was she as lonely

    as me? But we just stood there

smiling blindly, and the smell

    of those bags – heavy and sweet.

The Golden Thread

Sunday afternoons I prepare for birth by listening
to a CD where a sugary voice tells me
my breath is a golden thread floating

from my mouth into the distance, that a baby
is a golden ball of light, and my mind must learn
to be quiet for a good delivery.

And she never once says pain
but *waves, strength, pressure.*
And whatever your father is doing

soon he's asleep on the old floral sofa,
his face all misty and dreamy
while my mind chatters louder and louder

and your body wakes up to party
on my inside skin. I swear I can hear everything
but what this woman wants to tell me –

a chorus of far-off toilets flushing,
the side-gate creaking on its hinges –
why can't I see a golden thread floating

from my mouth? Instead the ghost-faces
of old boyfriends arise and I replay
our spiteful conversations, but when I open my eyes,

I'm blinded by the light, three bold sunrays
on the rug, and your father's face so utterly peaceful.
Then I see through the window the Jamaican guy

from the safe house has sat on our wall,
two litres of cider lifted skyward like a bugle.

Wood Green Stories
after Iain Crichton Smith

A boy from Lithuania
keeping a cat
to kill rats

                Small flags
                in windows –
                save our homes

Three girls
high heels
a tampered kebab

                The yellow tandem
                decked in plastic flowers
                outside Lidl

A feud between
one Evangelical church
and another

        Tropical fish
        in the storeroom
        of Matalan

Homeless man
with BHS boxed
dinner-set at his feet

        A female skeleton
        waiting three years
        on a bedsit settee

A romance
between
a fox and a waitress

        The longest
        Shellac nails
        in London

                Six silent men
                drinking pints
                at dawn

A tragedy
called
Flying Ant Day

Skirting

Now Rory rides these streets in his battered pram,
sat like a prophet, his milky arms spread open,
face-first into the world. So all things come
at him – chihuahuas, labradors, fat pigeons,
old leaves and chicken bones and summer rain,
sad toddlers in their own worn cars. But he holds
the chaps away – you see that nice young man
bowling towards us, snug jeans and smiling, bold
as brass? He couldn't touch me if he wanted,
my lad would keep him back – my cavalier
in corduroy and a bobble hat. He's chalked
a magic ring, a Mum-and-Rorysphere.
So all the fellows skirt us, dodge his slap,
but my own small fellow loves me – yes, there's that.

Total Body Conditioning

Before Pilates and Bikram and Zumba,
there was you, Mark, aerobics instructor
with a side-line in Kung Fu

and in that sprung-floored glass room
high over Brixton, the steam crept across the mirror
to frame us around you like backing singers –

on one side the black women
in their Jamaica colours, the white girls
in their pastels on the other

but when you kicked, we kicked, when you punched,
so we did too, punching no-one but ourselves,
left jab, right hook, uppercut.

The lycra you wore looked peel on, peel off,
not cloth but a second meniscal skin
you worked a sweat up in, the gleam

of gold on your wrists, a thick chain around
your thick strong neck. You shouted our names
like you owned us – *Latisha, Angela, Hannah!*

*

You played the same track over
and over: Sandy Rivera singing
And now my life is going through some changes

though nothing ever changed in that hour –
always the same zealous routine.
Mark, when that squelchy bassline kicked in

and we got to leaping and spinning,
I felt the same heart flurry
I'd felt twenty years before –

an elation both communal and solitary,
amphetamines rushing through me
in a warehouse behind Kings Cross,

a thousand hands in a rainbow strobe,
a boy pulling his top off,
that needle drop, that dance.

*

Before health and safety and risk assessment,
you'd run us out the Rec doors
and down the old iron steps
to Brixton Market, trains clattering overhead,
past the fish stalls – goby gaping on ice,
the stacks of plantain and cassava,
the stink of the butcher, meat swinging
on hooks. Brixton was mutating –
a chalk board boasted duck eggs,
smashed avos, flat whites – all a bit flat
and who knows what the old traders thought
of that, or thirty women chasing you
down Electric Avenue
like some crazed Pied Piper.

*

I carried the class timetable like a bible
because I couldn't stop smoking,
because I'd watched my father dying
and my mother's body failing her
so completely, I believed exercise
could stave off the thug who lurked
in my daily thoughts. When I bused
down the hill on Sunday mornings,
past the lush-eyed ravers of George IV
I felt some virtue or redemption
and besides, you made me laugh, Mark –
wheeler-dealer of the martial arts.
Patrizia of Body Pump was good but dour,
Donna's choreography was better, but you
were the best, making us scissor-kick
the air, squat and pump until our thighs
shook, then a hundred star jumps

*

My niece, who's moved to Brixton,
tells me of a fitness class she's found –
a killer, she says, *all punches and kicks*

and this crazy guy who shouts at us –
which is how I know you're still there,
south of the river, where my old life

still runs in time with this gentler one –
no cigarettes now, some yoga,
the small joyful boy I mother.

I saw you last on my old street,
you in your hoodie and jeans,
flirt and chancer,

licking my name in your mouth,
inviting yourself in for tea,
eyes locked on mine

like some small victory. Strange
to see you in your ordinaries,
I preferred you in that close second skin,

how I think of you now, your body older
and stronger, still dancing in the heart of the mirror,
that one gold tooth still glinting.

The Garden is Not for Everyone

All summer the children have been running **in the global refugee crisis** in the communal garden **Ammar is searching for his brother on a train** kicking a football through the yellow roses, chasing **the bodies roll out** across the parched ground **on the platform, a woman lifts a card sign** I hear their cries from the fourth floor *help us, save our souls!* A child on my side of the block & some days **who looks like my child is asleep** I take my boy down there to play **in the calm waters of a tourist beach** with Luna's boys – Albert, Adam, Ali **the newspapers don't know how** they live on the council side. Luna is Ethiopian I think **this story ends** & I mean to ask her when I see her down on our street **but describe the** baby bound in batik on her chest, but instead **smell of 71 people dead** we talk about the letter in her mailbox: **in a truck on the highway. We** the council children can no longer use **sincerely wish we could help** the communal garden – there is no reason **in the global refugee crisis**

Balconies

Because she complains about the water dripping through the slats
when I hose the plants, I complain about her cigarette smoke rising
and floating through our lounge.

We need these plants, I write, for oxygen, in all this pollution.
I would not have mentioned this, I write, out of neighbourliness,
had you not struck the first blow. I do not write 'first blow'.

Nor do I say how I often kneel among the greenery to watch her,
a bird's-eye slice of her body, the black roots of her hair
and the cigarette she sucks while speaking on the phone
to her mother in Romanian – *da Mamma, nu Mamma.*
The way she stares silently at the offices opposite,
her cigarette forgotten in the ashtray.

I will give up soon, she writes. I do not know the solution.
I hope we are not on bad terms. I mean this.

Outside June heats up, hotter than any I remember,
someone vomits in the lift, a wild man sleeps
in the basement, mice run up the exterior wall.

I'm glad to hear, I write. I stand above her now.
I try to resist looking down.

Multi-Storey

What do I tell my son about the car park across the street,
about the people we pass at its reeking gate –

the beautiful boy with cold sores, circling slowly on his scooter,
the grease-haired guy with yellow bongos slung on his shoulder?

When I'm on my own, I imagine climbing the stairs,
over the old syringes my neighbour tells me are there,

finding the girls he says are sprawled undressed on the top floor,
who call out to him as he unlocks his car.

From our balcony at night, I squint my eyes, stare out,
see nothing but the empty levels, concrete pillars, gold security light.

Now it's summer, the bongo-guy kneels outside with a cake tin,
bongos in lap, beating the whole of his life on the drum skin.

I can't help but think of the phrase – *singing for his supper.*
But he's easy to ignore, not like the Aztec panpipers

who hop around the pigeons, or those three boys
in caps and hi tops, body-popping like mechanical toys.

Yesterday, when we came past, he was topless and gaunt,
sweat running in bright rivulets. I could count each rib. I could count

the coppers in his tin. My son pulled my hand and pointed,
Mum, look at that man. Why is he wet? Why is he naked?

The cold sore boy scooted around him in figures of eight,
raised a tattooed finger, beckoned us towards the car park gate.

The River

I dreamt of living in a boat on the river
like once I'd seen: a marina behind the town
with oaks and greenstone sculptures, the soft mirror
of water, and nesting between two boats, a swan.
But when I returned, there were no swans or oaks,
just miles of coloured boats, their rusted flanks
colliding, and the breeze stank, and the water choked
with rats, where children dipped their cans and drank.
And in one cabin window, I saw my mother,
her mouth the shape of my name, and in another,
I saw my son, his face pressed to the pane,
a yellow car in his palm. And the wild sky rained
its horrible rain. And on the riverside
my father stood, and hugged his bones and cried.

The Dice

If there's anything I'd save in a fire
it's that pair of Roman ox-bone dice,
green with age, fished, the antiquarian said,
from the Thames gut – what the river
sucks down, it spits back up. Gift of a lover –
thoughtful, considered, they carry me back
to my father: dice man, chancer,
forty years in England, trying his luck.

My son loves those dice,
sneaks them from my drawer and runs through
our flat, dice gripped in his small hot palm.
He cries when I unpeel them, like he knows
their power, but can't yet name it, the way
he knows the flowers outside the local cinema
stand for sadness. How can I tell him, it's there,
nearly random, one boy shot dead another?

Deportation Blues

From small and airless rooms,
they are taken, handcuffed, to silver coaches –
the ex-soldier, the diabetic, the boy who came aged three.
The aeroplane leaves at dawn.

They are taken in silver cuffs
with black-coat escorts on either side.
The aeroplane leaves at dawn.
They are body-belted to their seats

with black-coat escorts either side –
security guards on hourly rates
who body-belt them to their seats,
the man who struggles and shouts

until the guard on hourly rates
closes his hands around his head
until the man cannot struggle or shout.
The one who drops his head in prayer,

closing his hands around his head.
He has six children, three under five,
the one who drops his head in prayer
and two convictions for weed, for speeding.

He has six children, three under five.
He can't remember Clarendon, Jamaica
but two convictions for weed, for speeding.
They deport you for this.

He can't remember Above Rocks, Jamaica,
the young one who grew up in care.
They deport you for this.
I need to get back to my son, believe me

the one who grew up in Hebden Bridge.
After the fingerprints, the interview –
I need to get back to my son, believe me
It's my little daughter's birthday.

After the paperwork, the interview,
the one who grew up in Barkingside.
it was my little daughter's birthday.
Up all night to phone his wife, his children,

the one who grew up in Barkingside.
In these airless downtown rooms,
up all night to phone their wives, children, home –
the ex-soldier, the diabetic, the boy who came aged three.

Paper Work

Gambling man ain't pay no national insurance. Red passport went in a burglary.
Blue passport shows a younger man this old man squints to see – *it say that me?*

Behind the flash-bulb face, he still remembers – heart full of wicked father,
no-see mother, hurricane. And England calling like a damsel, *help me?*

Surely this drawer will spill belonging – old gas bill, playing cards, green rizla –
a horse tip biro'ed on the rim. Wonder if that horse came in.

Now the dog's behind him in the road – this 30-year-old stroll with one dog or another.
A newspaper from Singh's, best piece of back bacon the butcher wraps for him,

prescriptions from the chemist, now his heart's gone weak. Then walking back
to search some more. In dreams, he hears them banging on his door –

he comes at them with playing cards and rizla, his notebooks scrawled with horses' odds.
They lock the dog he loves in a cage – her crying and whining.

These turned leaves underfoot, the paving stones his daughter used to jump
the cracks across, this funeral rain. Home feels like this.

And now they say the country isn't his?

The Trucks

We heard them pulling up, the barking voices,
a woman in the street – Irina? – putting up
a fight. Each night, the bell's insistent buzz,
the foot-stomps on the stairs. My boy in my lap,
I sat in darkness, two fingers pressed to his lips.
We heard their boots kick open the landing door
then cries. Each night that week, they came for more

      until our long white corridor was silent
      and those flats were boarded shut. I had not known
      there were so many. Half the building went.
      Half the city. We just made out their ringing phones.
      Someone said something about a holding zone
      but where? We whispered their names – Danuta, Jan,
      the baby Roza; Junko and her mad Italian;

a couple I'd never spoken to, who'd pinned
a blue eye to their door. Somebody said
the men were handcuffed, there was a field of planes.
The radio played endless pop ballads,
our telly flashed its messages in red
between the sitcom re-runs and Pathé films.
More news to come. Please stay at home. Stay calm.

      Days later, they ordered children back to school.
      I walked my boy across the muted streets
      to Miss Powell with her swollen eyes and bell
      and the children waiting on the chalky asphalt,
      so few then – Amanda, Sarah, Rory, Paul –
      to be taken to their classroom, up the stairs,
      past the empty hooks, the stacks of plastic chairs.

Scooting

Now Rory wants to scoot on his own dammit,
to soar one-footed down the high street – who cares
about red lights or buses or the reckless cars?
You cars should watch it, else he'll mount your bonnet
and flick his wheels until his scooter whirls
like a helicopter blade on your old tin roof,
might even lift you, levitate a troupe
of cars into the sky, while the boys and girls
below look up to wave and call out *toodle-oo*
or kneel to aim their finger-guns. And when
you cars combust, a million curlicues
of car-dust will decorate the sky, and spin
around my boy, scooting on his own
between the stars and planets, across the moon...

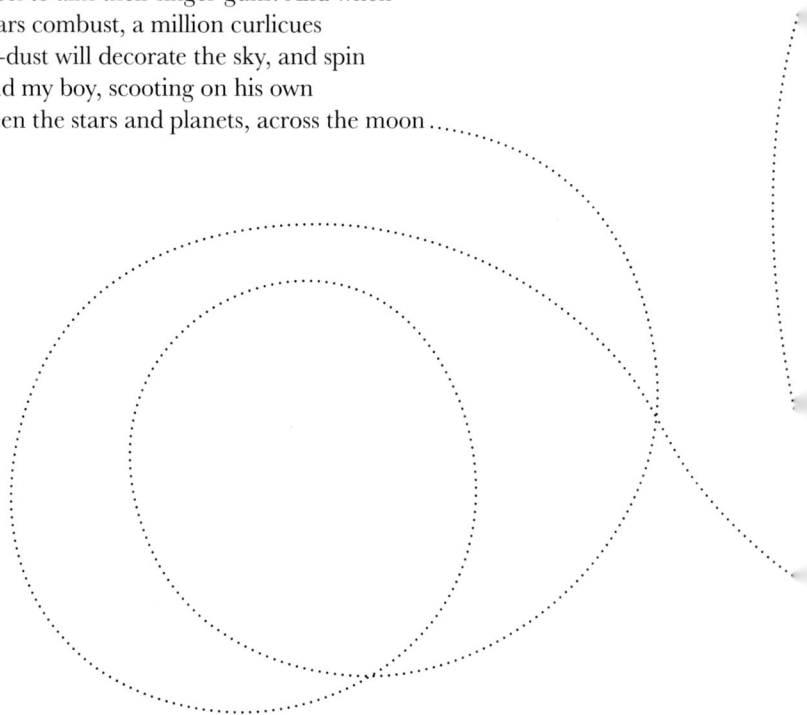